We the People

The Constitution and You

FREEDOM OF SPEECH

by Paul J. Deegan

Abdo & Daughters
Minneapolis

Published by Abdo & Daughters, 6537 Cecilia Circle, Bloomington, Minnesota 55435

Library bound edition distributed by Rockbottom Books, Pentagon Tower, P.O. Box 36036, Minneapolis, Minnesota 55435

Library of Congress Number: 87-071089   ISBN: 0-939179-22-9

Cover illustration by Elaine Wadsworth

Consultants:

Phyllis R. Abbott
Ph.D. — University of Wisconsin (Madison)
Professor of History
Mankato State University
Mankato, Minnesota

Bailey W. Blethen
J.D. — University of Minnesota Law School
Partner in law firm of Blethen, Gage & Krause
Mankato, Minnesota

Lewis H. Croce
Ph.D. — University of Maryland
Professor of History
Mankato State University
Mankato, Minnesota

The first 10 Amendments to the United States Constitution

The Bill of Rights

AMENDMENT 1

Congress shall make no law respecting an establishment of religion, or prohibiting the free exercise thereof; or abridging the freedom of speech, or of the press; or the right of the people peaceably to assemble, and to petition the government for a redress of grievances.

AMENDMENT 2

A well-regulated militia being necessary to the security of a free State, the right of the people to keep and bear arms shall not be infringed.

AMENDMENT 3

No soldier shall, in time of peace be quartered in any house without the consent of the owner, nor in time of war, but in a manner to be prescribed by law.

AMENDMENT 4

The right of the people to be secure in their persons, houses, papers and effects, against unreasonable searches and seizures, shall not be violated, and no warrants shall issue but upon probable cause, supported by oath or affirmation, and particularly describing the place to be searched, and the persons or things to be seized.

AMENDMENT 5

No person shall be held to answer for a capital or otherwise infamous crime, unless on a presentment or indictment of a grand jury, except in cases arising in the land or naval forces, or in the militia, when in actual service in time of war or public danger; nor shall any person be subject for the same offense to be twice put in jeopardy of life or limb; nor shall be compelled in any criminal case to be a witness against himself, nor be deprived of life, liberty, or property, without due process of law; nor shall private property be taken for public use, without just compensation.

AMENDMENT 6

In all criminal prosecutions, the accused shall enjoy the right to a speedy and public trial, by an impartial jury of the State and district wherein the crime shall have been committed, which district shall have been previously ascertained by law, and to be informed of the nature and cause of the accusation; to be confronted with the witnesses against him; to have compulsory process of obtaining witnesses in his favor, and to have the assistance of counsel for his defense.

AMENDMENT 7

In suits at common law, where the value in controversy shall exceed twenty dollars, the right of trial by jury, shall be preserved, and no fact tried by a jury shall be otherwise reexamined in any court of the United States than according to the rules of the common law.

AMENDMENT 8

Excessive bail shall not be required, nor excessive fines imposed, nor cruel and unusual punishments inflicted.

AMENDMENT 9

The enumeration in the Constitution of certain rights shall not be construed to deny or disparage others retained by the people.

AMENDMENT 10

The powers not delegated to the United States by the Constitution, nor prohibited by it to the States, are reserved to the States respectively, or to the people.

"We the People of the United States . . .establish this CONSTITUTION for the United States of America."

Freedom of speech — this is what Martin Luther King knew he had when he stood before 100,000 people in Washington, D.C., in the late summer of 1963. He lived in a country governed by a Constitution which insured him — and us — the right to free speech.

Across the country in Los Angeles five years later, a lone young man knew this too.

At that time a war was being fought by United States servicemen in a faraway place called Vietnam. The war made many people upset in the 1960s. Some were in favor of the war. Others very much opposed it.

Young men were being drafted to serve in the Army. Many of those who were drafted soon found themselves fighting in Vietnam.

On a spring day in 1968, the young man in Los Angeles was walking in a courthouse hallway. On his jacket was a vulgar message—obscene to some—regarding the draft.

The young man's name was Paul Robert Cohen. He later would say in court that he wore the jacket in the Los Angeles County courthouse knowing that the words were on it because he wanted to let the public know how much he was opposed to both the Vietnam War and the draft.

Because of the message on the jacket he was arrested for disturbing the peace. This crime would be called disorderly conduct in some states. Los Angeles authorities arrested him because they thought that wearing the jacket in a public place was offensive conduct.

Three years later, Cohen's arrest was the basis of a case being argued before the Supreme Court of the United States in Washington, D.C. On June 7, 1971, the court would make public its decision in this case.

The major issue before the court was whether the message on the jacket was an exercise of free speech protected by the 1st Amendment to the Constitution of the United States.

The Supreme Court's decision would relate the Constitution to you . . .

The right to express what you want without fear of being punished by local, state, or national governments is cherished by Americans.

When Americans talk about their rights, they usually mean the basic liberties protected by the Constitution in the Bill of Rights, the first 10 amendments.

The first nine amendments were the work of James Madison, a Founding Father of the United States. Madison played a major role in the development of the Constitution and its approval by the states.

James Madison

He continued his direct involvement with the nation's guiding law in his work on the Bill of Rights.

The first 10 amendments were ratified or approved by the states and went into effect in 1791. At the time they applied only to the federal (national) government.

The Bill of Rights did not apply to the states. States could, and did, have laws which limited basic rights.

It was some 180 years after the Bill of Rights was ratified before the Supreme Court really began applying it to situations involving citizens and their relationships with state governments.

The full application of the Bill of Rights to women was not made until court cases in the 1970s.

14TH AMENDMENT

The basis for applying the protection of the Bill of Rights to incidents on a state level is the 14th Amendment, which went into effect in 1868.

"Nor shall any state," reads the last part of the 14th Amendment, "deprive any person of life, liberty, or property without due process of law; nor deny to any person within its jurisdiction the equal protection of the laws."

More than 40 years before the incident in the California courthouse, the language was cited by the Supreme Court in a landmark decision. That decision involved a case where free speech was also the issue. The court said that language in the 14th Amendment meant that freedom of speech could not be restricted by a state.

Thus, the 14th Amendment was used as the vehicle to apply the protections of the First Amendment to a state case.

Therefore, in 1971 Paul Cohen, the man who had been arrested in the courthouse, argued that the California law under which he was convicted violated his rights to freedom of expression. This freedom, he said, was guaranteed him by the 1st and 14th Amendments to the Constitution.

Cohen's arrest, conviction, and sentence to 30 days in jail was a commonplace event in any city's municipal court system.

Most such events end right there. However, Cohen was able to protest his arrest through a series of courts until his arguments were being heard by the highest court in the land.

He was able to do so because the Constitution, written nearly 200 years before, both set up a court system which allowed for review and set forth in the Bill of Rights and the 14th Amendment a guarantee that basic rights are to be protected.

"The measure of an advanced civilization is how it treats its worst people, not its best." That is the opinion of another Californian who contested his conviction for a minor crime all the way to the Supreme Court.

SUPREME COURT

Court of Appeals

Trial Court

However, not every one who believes their rights have been violated gets a hearing before the Supreme Court. The requests to the high court are far more than it could ever handle. Some 5,000 cases a year are submitted for review. Less than 200 will be selected to be heard. That's less than 4 of every 100.

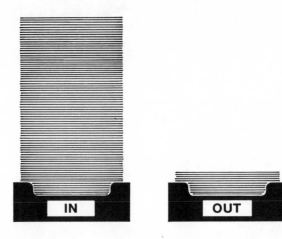

Those cases which the court selects to hear are cases which, in the opinion of the Supreme Court justices, deal with important fundamental issues. (Congress has established the right to appeal cases where a federal statute is overturned by a lower court.)

So Paul Cohen was unusual or, some might say, lucky, or, more likely, the justices saw the major issue in his case as one which went to the heart of the matter of freedom of speech.

That issue, as the court would analyze the case, was the protection of unpopular or even offensive speech.

Once the high court decided the Cohen appeal was one it wanted to consider, the case became part of a rather formalized process followed by the court.

The process includes written briefs — statements of positions — by attorneys for both sides. The attorneys also come to Washington for oral "arguments" — they appear before the justices where the attorneys make oral presentations and answer questions submitted by the justices. The court itself researches the case. This includes reviewing previously-decided decisions which relate to the case being appealed.

Young lawyers serving as clerks to the Supreme Court justices participate in the research. A position as clerk is eagerly sought by many top law school graduates.

A key part of the process in an appeal is a conference of the Supreme Court justices. These regularly scheduled discussions usually take place on Wednesday afternoons and Friday mornings from October to about the first of July.

By custom, the justices begin these conferences in the Supreme Court Building in Washington by shaking hands with each other. No one is in the room other than the justices. The Chief Justice speaks first.

He generally will outline a case. Then he will state his position. Will he vote to sustain or support the appeal? This is not a final position, but it may very well remain the same when a decision is eventually issued.

Then each of the other justices states his or her position. This is done in the order of their seniority on the court. When they have all spoken, the outcome is at least tentatively decided.

One of the justices is assigned to put in writing the court's decision and the reasoning for it. This written explanation is called an "opinion". If the Chief Justice is on the majority side, he chooses the justice who will write the opinion. If not, the senior justice on the majority side makes the assignment.

Those on the minority side — the losing side if you will — are called "dissenters". They often write an opinion presenting their position. Sometimes, justices dissent for different reasons. Then there may be more than one dissenting opinion.

It is unusual for there to be a 9-0 vote for or against the appealed decision. Since there are nine justices, there can be no ties if no seat is vacant.

Now the opinion or opinions are drafted. Clerks might participate in the drafting. During the drafting and rewriting of an opinion, the justices might exchange written comments and questions. Some might even change their position.

When the justices in the majority approve a final draft of an opinion, it is dated and released to the public. The decision has been issued. The decisions always are released on Fridays.

The majority opinion in *Cohen versus California* was written by Justice John Harlan. He expressed the views of the justices in the majority in this five-to-four decision.

Justice Harlan noted that "This case may seem at first blush too inconsequential to find its way into our books. . ."

However, he said, the issue was a very important one. Justice Harlan wrote that ". . .the issue it presents is of no small constitutional significance."

The case was "very important" because it dealt with protecting expression of words — speech in the terms of the basic right even though no spoken words were at issue in this case — which some or even many people find unpleasant or even offensive.

The opinion reviewed the facts in the case. Cohen said nothing in the courthouse. He did not make any loud or unusual noises. He did not commit any act of violence. He did not threaten to do so.

So what was his offensive conduct for which he was convicted in the Los Angeles Municipal Court?

The California Court of Appeal had defined "offensive conduct" as "behavior which has a tendency to provoke *others* to acts of violence or to in turn disturb the peace."

Cohen had appealed his municipal court conviction to that court. The California Court of Appeal had affirmed or upheld Cohen's conviction. The court said the state had proved offensive conduct in municipal court.

Cohen's conduct — putting the message on his jacket — might very well, the court said, cause others "to commit a violent act against (Cohen). . .or attempt to forceably remove his jacket."

The case was appealed to the United State Supreme Court after the California Supreme Court refused to review it. This, in effect, left stand the original conviction.

So what does the nation's highest court consider when a citizen argues in 1971 that a right guaranteed him under the Constitution's Bill of Rights, written 182 years earlier in 1789, has been denied him or her?

Obviously, James Madison, who drafted the 1st Amendment, did not have in mind a war in southeast Asia or a military draft.

When the Supreme Court takes a case such as Cohen's, it has seen a particular question it thinks should be addressed in terms of:

What does the Constitution mean in this particular situation?

To come to an answer, the court often breaks the situation into several parts. It may raise questions about several things.

In *Cohen versus California* the court determined, for one thing, that Cohen's conviction in Los Angeles Municipal Court rested on the claim that the words on his jacket were offensive.

The only conduct the state wanted to punish, the majority opinion says, was "the fact of communication." Referring to a case decided 40 years earlier, the court said the conviction thus rested solely upon "speech".

"Speech protected from . . . Governmental Interference"

More so, the court said, Cohen's conviction rested ". . .squarely upon his execise of the 'freedom of speech' protected from arbitrary governmental interference by the Constitution. . ."

So, the court reasoned, the conviction ". . .can be justified, if at all, only as a valid regulation of the manner in which he exercised that freedom. . ."

Thus, the issue then, according to the court, was not the message itself.

However, the court noted that neither the 1st nor the 14th Amendments have ever been "thought to give absolute protection to every individual to speak whenever or wherever he pleases. . ."

The limitations courts have placed on freedom of speech include, for example, "fighting words" (words likely to provoke a violent reaction), shouting "fire" in a crowded theater, and obscenity.

In the Cohen opinion, the court said "This is not . . . an obscenity case."

For states to forbid obscene expression, Justice Harlan wrote, the expression or speech in question ". . .must be, in some significant way, erotic." In other words, the speech in question must tend to arouse sexual desire. This would not result from reading the message on Cohen's jacket, the court said.

The opinion said the four-letter word displayed by Cohen relating to the draft is sometimes used to provoke someone. In this instance, however, the word "was clearly not" directed at any specific person, the court said.

"No individual actually or likely to be present could reasonably have regarded the words on appellant's

(Cohen's) jacket as a direct personal insult." the opinion said. Nor, it said, was it shown that anyone who saw Cohen became upset or that Cohen intended to provoke anyone.

The opinion says California authorities claimed the state had a right to protect "the sensitive" who might unavoidably see Cohen's "crude form of protest."

FIGHTING WORDS

For one thing, the court said, the possibility that someone may accidentally see or hear something does not automatically justify forbidding ". . .speech capable of giving offense." The opinion noted that the court has ". . .consistently stressed that 'we are often "captives" outside the . . .home and subject to objectionable speech.' "

To limit speech just to protect others from hearing it, the court said, it must be shown that there is a serious invasion of the protected person's right to privacy.

Otherwise, the court said, a majority could effectively silence protestors simply because they felt like it.

The court, therefore, held that "if Cohen's 'speech' was otherwise entitled to constitutional protection," the fact that someone in a public building — the courthouse — unwillingly happened to see the message on the jacket does not justify his conviction for disturbing the peace.

Another factor to be considered, the court said, was whether states "may properly remove this offensive word from the public vocabulary" while "acting as guardians of public morality."

The Cohen opinion said the "usual rule" is that government may not regulate "the form or content of individual expression."

"Equally important to our conclusion is the constitutional backdrop against which our decision must be made.

"Free expression is powerful medicine."

"The constitutional right of free expression is powerful medicine in a society as diverse and populous as ours.

"It is designed and intended" to allow public discussion to take place without restrictions by any form of government.

This is done, the opinion said, in order to put ". . .the decision as to what views shall be voiced largely into the hands of each of us, in the hope that use of such freedom will ultimately produce a more capable citizenry. . ."

The court took note that many would see this freedom resulting only in conflict or offensive speech. The court said any such results were "necessary side effects of the broader enduring values which the process of open debate permits us to achieve."

That offensive, foolish, insensitive or downright unwise speech is permitted is, the court said, "not a sign of weakness but of strength." The opinion cited another decision of the court which said "so long as the means are peaceful, the communication need not meet standards of acceptability."

The high court asked how one would be able to distinguish the one word used by Cohen from any other offensive word. It said the state doesn't have the right to cleanse speech in public to the extent that it is acceptable to "the most squeamish among us."

The word of concern in this case, the court said, "is perhaps more distasteful than most other of its genre (type)." But, the opinion said, "it is nevertheless often true that one man's vulgarity is another's lyric."

The Constitution thus generally "leaves matters of taste and style. . .to the individual."

Also, Justice Harlan wrote, speech sometimes serves two purposes. It conveys ideas in some detail. It also may express emotions. "In fact, words are often chosen as much for their emotive as (for) their cognitive (being capable of expressing knowledge) force," he said.

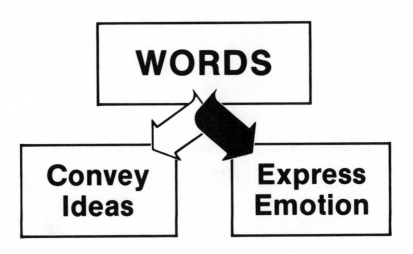

The final part of the question as posed by the court majority was what might happen if government could forbid particular words? Their answer was that the result could be a high risk that ideas also would be suppressed.

"Indeed," the opinion said, "governments might soon seize upon the censorship of particular words as a covenient guise (excuse) for banning the expression of unpopular views."

These, then, were the views of the Supreme Court in 1971 as it presented its reasoning for the decision it was going to make in *Cohen versus California*.

Do you think you know what the court's decision was?

The court concluded that under the 1st and 14th Amendments the state of California may not "make the simple public display of this single four-letter expletive a criminal offense."

The court reversed Paul Cohen's conviction.

He was no longer a criminal.

His crime had been minor, but he had believed he was only expressing a right he had as an American citizen.

It had been a trivial incident in which he was involved. His protest no doubt would have been quickly forgotten if he had not been arrested.

Instead the incident had resulted in a significant Supreme Court decision.

The Constitution had guaranteed Paul Cohen — and all of us — the freedom of speech.

The Constitution had created the court which had the final say about Paul Cohen's conviction.

That court reemphasized an American's right to criticize actions of his or her government. That protection extends beyond informed and responsible criticism. The Constitution, the court said, protects critical speech even when it is unpopular, controversial, or offensive.